MICHAEL SMITH'S
POSH NOSH BOOK

D1798429

Michael Smith, known to *Pebble Mill's* viewers for his weekly cookery spot, *Grace and Flavour,* went last summer with director Desmond Lapsley and a BBC film unit to take a look at some of England's top cooks.

Their objective was to show visually not only the type of establishment these perfectionists ran, but, more important, how they set about it and how their personal philosophies differed from those of other restaurateurs and hotel-keepers. These restaurants are showered with stars by the world's major food guides; the tables have to be booked weeks, if not months, in advance and any self-respecting food writer must have wined and dined there to feel in the swim of food trends.

Yet, with one exception, these cooks all started with another career. None had undergone a formal training of the type our educationalists deem necessary before entering the catering business. They are 'gifted amateurs', who, through sheer hard work, have reached the top, usually breaking all the rules in the professional book *en route.*

As Michael Smith suspected, one thing was quite clear: there is no short cut to this kind of success. But in spite of the gruelling hours, the early financial struggles, and the hard work, none would return to his or her former career.

Although this book can only give a limited insight into the lives of these people, it does offer some superlative dishes you can make at home.

Raspberry Sauce, Brown Sauce and Hollandaise Sauce are from Michael Smith's *Saucy Cookbook* published by the BBC.

Published by the British Broadcasting Corporation, 35 Marylebone High Street, London W1M 4AA

ISBN 0 563 17701 2
First published 1979
© Michael Smith 1979

Printed in England by
The Yale Press, London SE25.

INTRODUCTION

There are schools and colleges in England which offer grades of cooking training from a Bachelor's Degree in Hotel Administration to National Diplomas obtainable after some three or more years' training. There are also many part-time courses which almost anyone can attend to gain at least some knowledge about the cooking business. It is strange, then, that a hotel or restaurant owner has to search hard to find a cook or waiter who is capable of combining food ingredients with grace and flavour or who can set a fork and glass on a table with even a modicum of individual flair.

Most of these restaurant owners prefer to train their staff members from scratch, untouched by school or college. Only then are they able to pass on the secrets of their own skills. Some believe that a few colleges are, in principle, a good thing but that they often produce inflexible and therefore untrainable cooks.

Let me set down the essential qualities which the great chefs of this book consider necessary for the aspiring cook, waiter or receptionist to acquire before they can become good restaurateurs. These are simple and require no great training — nothing but an urgent desire to get into the trade.

Cooks and Chefs
A need to cook. A keen eye and sensitive palate. Energy. Single-mindedness. A desire to eat well, for how can one cook if one has never known what it is to eat well? A mind open to new ideas. Dedication.

Waiters, Barmen and Receptionists
Style and charm, both of which can, to some extent, be acquired. An almost obsessive attention to personal appearance. A desire to please. Belief in good food. Dedication. Individualism — even when part of a team.

Age doesn't matter in the restaurant business but self-knowledge does. If you are in any doubt as to whether or not you should enter the hotel and restaurant trade, then the answer is *don't*. You will not make a success of it. The number who are succeeding, however, is happily on the increase in 1979.

This book stresses the attention to detail which top

3

restaurateurs devote to both the front and the back-of-house in well-run establishments. Culinary ingredients are of the best quality. There is always a choice between salted and unsalted butter. Black or white milled pepper, at least three sorts of home baked bread, and iced water is always provided. There are tissues in the cloakrooms. Half-filled, small bowls of titbits are always kept topped up, and, believe it or not, dead flowers and fallen leaves are tidied up hourly! Fires blaze in the winter and in the summer the grates are attractively shielded or filled with foliage. Any magazines are current and curtains are drawn on grey days. Lights are carefully grouped and switched on at all times. It is house-keeping on a truly magnificent scale.

Most successful restaurants are captained by their owners, either from their kitchens, or from a front-of-house vantage point where an eye can be kept on the whole show. Successful owners realise that not only must the customer be satisfied but the staff must also be content in their work. Ideally, a second person should be involved. Two heads *are* better than one, but it is important for each to make an individual contribution. It was delightful to find that no two places were the same. Each had its own style, and charm and a certain magic which stems from human creativity.

Every successful restaurateur has worked long hours, devoted himself wholeheartedly to his venture and given encouragement and unstinted tuition to apprentices. These enterprising people are now being rewarded but then so are all guests who eat at their tables.

I hope these pages give some idea of their food and their philosophies.

Michael Smith

WHITE MOSS HOUSE

Ten years ago Arthur Butterworth was a commercial financial director in Lancashire's industrial Rawtenstall Valley, and his wife, Jean, was a senior mistress in a large school. After much debate they decided that they would abandon the rat-race and retire to the part of England which they loved best — the Lake District. However, two considerations arose. Money would prove to be a problem if they were to continue to enjoy their accustomed life-style, and Jean, a creative woman, would be left with no outlet for her abilities. Climbing mountains all day would not be the solution.

Their decision to purchase White Moss House solved this dilemma and completely changed the direction of their lives. The eighteenth-century manor house, which nestles in a mountain side, overlooks Rydal Water and is only a few minutes' walk from Wordsworth's Grasmere. It proved to be an ideal house in which to start a restaurant. Determined not to create an enterprise involving either children or industry this time, they decided from the start that White Moss should be run single handed with only a little help from local women in nearby villages.

This home from home offers every comfort the Lakeland guest could want, but its chief virtue is that it enables him or her to sample Jean's superb food. At 8 p.m. in the softly lit dining-room the crystal sparkles, the silver glistens and Arthur moves imperceptibly between the tables while the eighteen guests, never more never less, sit down for dinner. Eighteen guests is their maximum and nothing will persuade them to exceed the number, a brave policy when they know that they could fill the house twice over, so great is the demand for the traditional English flavour of Jean's cooking. This quality is really present in their breakfast platter of Cumberland sausage, sweet-cured bacon, eggs, tomatoes, mushrooms, fried breads and, for the hearty appetite, a goodly slice of delicious black pudding. It is also found in their elaborate game dishes when in season, and in the simple, but delicious home-made oatmeal biscuit served with a rich port-laden potted cheese and a crisp Granny Smith apple.

Breads for breakfast, cakes for afternoon tea and biscuits by your bedside come daily from Jean's kitchen. The making

5

JEAN & ARTHUR BUTTERWORTH

of chutneys, jams, jellies and marmalades keeps her busy in the winter. An abundant herb garden grows outside her door and their flavours enrich her soups and sauces and pervade her salads and vegetables, just as they did in the eighteenth century when White Moss was built. The garden takes up much of Jean and Arthur's time but it gives pleasure to the visitor's eye as well as contributing towards flavouring the food.

When I asked Arthur how he likes being a waiter, constantly attending the public, he looked to his pretty wife and said, 'If I wasn't sure that each of Jean's dishes would be perfectly cooked I could never do it.' Many places claim that guests will be looked after as if they were at home, but these claims are often hollow. Not so at the Butterworths, for it *is* their home and you share not only its cosy rooms and charming views of the Lakeland hills but you also share that unique third dimension — their pleasure in working together.

WHITE MOSS HOUSE

Egg with Avocado Mayonnaise
Fresh Salmon Braid
Beetroot au Gratin
Gingered Pears
Potted Stilton
Oatmeal Biscuits

Egg with Avocado Mayonnaise

1 avocado pear	Salt and pepper
1 egg	Lumpfish roe (optional)
Juice of $\frac{1}{2}$ lemon	6 tbsp olive oil

Cut the pear, which must be ripe, in half, and remove stone. Scoop out the flesh and put into a blender with whole egg and lemon juice. Blend until really smooth. Put oil into a jug and *slowly* pour through the hole in the blender lid with the machine running at slow speed. When mixed, season to taste with salt and pepper. Place a hard-boiled egg, sliced lengthways, on a bed of lettuce, spoon mayonnaise over and decorate with a little black lumpfish roe.

Garnish with watercress and sliced black olives. Serve with thinly-cut wholemeal bread and butter.

This recipe makes enough Avocado Mayonnaise for 6 servings.

Fresh Salmon Braid

8 oz home-made puff pastry	Mace
1 lb cold poached salmon	Egg wash
$\frac{1}{4}$ pint rich Béchamel sauce	
$\frac{1}{2}$ small cucumber,	
de-seeded but not peeled	
1 tbsp chopped parsley or	
other fresh herbs	

Roll out pastry thinly into a rectangle. Leave to rest while preparing the filling. Frozen puff pastry can be used.

Flake salmon and remove any skin and bones. Mix with parsley and Béchamel sauce. Chop the de-seeded cucumber into quarter-inch dice. Put a layer of cucumber down centre of pastry. Top with salmon mixture and dust lightly with powdered mace. Cut diagonal slits at half-inch intervals in pastry on either side of, and up to, the filling. Brush down outer edges with egg wash and fold over filling, taking a strip alternately from each side. Brush with egg wash, being careful not to coat cut edges. Put in cool place to rest. Bake in hot oven, gas mark 7, 425°F, until well risen and golden brown — about 30 minutes. Serve hot with new potatoes, garden peas and a cucumber salad dressed with sour cream and chives.

Beetroot au Gratin

Wash the unpeeled beetroot well, and cook in salted water until tender. Peel and dice into a shallow fireproof dish. Coat thinly with Béchamel sauce, and top with wholemeal breadcrumbs. Dot with butter and place in a hot oven to reheat the beetroot and brown the crumbs.

Gingered Pears

4 ripe William pears	½ cup Advocaat
½ pint double cream	Stem ginger and syrup

Peel and dice pears into a stemmed glass and trickle a little ginger syrup over them. Make a ginger syllabub by whipping cream and Advocaat until thick and soft. Fold in chopped ginger and spoon over pears. Top with a slice of ginger. Serve with home-made ginger biscuits or brandysnaps.

Potted Stilton

8 oz stilton (can be the very ripe left-overs, grate it if it is firm)	8 oz unsalted butter (softened at room temperature)
Port	Mace

Mix stilton and butter together (a food processor is ideal for this). Add port up to 3 tbsp and mix well. Pot and top with powdered mace.

Oatmeal Biscuits

¼ lb plain flour	3 oz lard
½ lb oats (porridge, not oat meal)	½ tsp salt
3 oz castor sugar	½ tsp bicarbonate of soda
3 oz margarine	A little milk

Sieve flour with salt and bicarbonate of soda. Rub fat into flour and oats. Add sugar and mix with milk and make a firm dough. Roll out thinly and cut into rounds. Bake on a greased tray, gas mark 6, 400°F, until light golden (10 minutes).

Serve to be 'buttered' with cheese.

COLIN LONG & MALCOLM REID

THE BOX TREE RESTAURANT

The West Yorkshire town of Ilkley was for decades famous for two things: Ilkley Moor of the famous song and the Roman Springs where wealthy Victorians and Edwardians tried to cure their aches and pains. The spa town is now a pleasant dormitory for the nearby metropolitan giant cities of Leeds and Bradford and the bustling towns of Huddersfield and Halifax.

Some eighteen years ago, seeds were sewn for a venture which was to add a third dimension to the town of Ilkley and put it on the international map. Two young men, surfeited with Yorkshire pudding, bought a small seventeenth-century cottage in Church Street. What started life as little more than an 'Olde English Tea Shoppe' was to become, within a few short years of hard work and hard-won experience, a restaurant of such fame that even the French awarded it two stars in the prestigious *Michelin Food Guide*. This was high praise indeed from the French, and in those days it was the only restaurant outside London to receive such an accolade. Now Americans and Latin Americans, Japanese and Javanese, flock to The Box Tree Restaurant to wine and dine with Malcolm Reid and Colin Long.

Outside, next to the large white front door in Church Street, is fixed a plain brass plate which inscribes simply: M Reid, C Long, Restaurateurs. This symbolises both their outrageous style in décor and, more important, their chaste dedication to the food served.

Inside, every corner of The Box Tree is filled with an abundance of flowers — not sophisticated arrangements, but massed blooms and plants as natural as the herbaceous borders of an English garden.

In the Yorkshire manner, evidence of pride and effort is manifest everywhere. Huge hand-hewn logs burn in each grate, brass and copper and silver gleam, abundant antiques glow from many years of polishing. Handsome paintings, mirrors, candelabra and costly *bric-à-brac* are dusted daily. At first glance the *mise en scène* seems too much — overdone even — but one soon realises that it is not camp, but stylish flamboyance. Each treasure has been lovingly bought and thoughtfully placed for the enjoyment of guests, and is an integral part of their very personal philosophy: that presentation and a sense of occasion is one

11

of the things the restaurant business is all about. Every night is a first night — every dish is a first creation. It becomes obvious that as much thought has gone into the construction of the daily menu as in the placing of the most valuable miniature on the velvet walls. Even Escoffier himself can be improved on at times — an observation which these inspired restaurateurs demonstrate!

They met at a tennis club in Leeds. At the time one of them was a shirt salesman and the other hawked gimmicky ties. It is plain that their sense of style has won them their huge success. It cannot be repressed. From buying in the market (being with them on such an expedition is in itself an exhausting though rewarding experience) to bidding goodnight to the replete and happy guest, everything and everybody undergoes the magic touch.

THE BOX TREE RESTAURANT

Crêpes Alfredo
Noisettes d'Agneau au Noilly
Haricots verts aux Fines Herbes
Tarte Amandine

Crêpes Alfredo

Filling

4-5 lb fresh spinach
6 tbsp melted butter
$\frac{3}{4}$ lb raw chicken (breast or legs)
2 small onions

$\frac{1}{2}$ clove garlic
$\frac{1}{4}$ pint double cream
Salt and freshly-ground black pepper

Crêpe Batter (pancake)

4 oz plain flour
$\frac{1}{2}$ pint milk

3 eggs
2 level tbsp melted butter

Cheese Sauce

3 oz butter
3 oz plain flour
2 pints milk
12 oz freshly-grated Parmesan cheese

Salt and freshly-ground white pepper

To make the filling

Wash spinach well, removing any yellowed or damaged leaves. Drain and then remove stalks. Sauté spinach leaves in a pan with 4 level tablespoons of the butter, stirring constantly, until spinach 'wilts'. Transfer to large sieve, press out liquid. Remove skin from chicken; cut meat into thin strips. Chop onions and garlic finely and sauté in 2 level tablespoons butter over a low heat, stirring from time to time, until onions are transparent. Add chicken meat and continue to cook, stirring until chicken is just tender. Remove from heat. Combine spinach and chicken and onion mixture and pass through the fine blade of a mincer (not a blender). Add cream and season.

To make batter

Combine flour, milk, eggs and melted butter in the bowl of an electric blender and blend well. Pour batter into a bowl and leave for at least half an hour before making the pancakes. When ready to fry pancakes, cover an upturned soup plate with a folded cloth. Heat a small heavy pancake pan about 6 inches diameter. When it is very hot, rub entire surface very lightly with a wad of kitchen paper moistened with oil. Pour about 2 tablespoons batter into centre of pan, tilting it quickly so that it coats bottom of pan very thinly. If you find you have too much batter, pour excess back into bowl once a thin layer has set on the bottom of the pan. Cook steadily for about a minute, drawing a spatula or the point of a knife round edges to loosen it. As soon as small bubbles begin to form under the pancake, flip it over and cook for another 60-90 seconds. Slip each one on to the prepared plate and cover with the cloth. Make 12 pancakes in this way with one or two reserves, stacking them on top of each other under a cloth. Oil pan lightly in between making each pancake.

To make sauce
Melt butter, stir in the flour and cook over a low heat, stirring constantly until a pale roux is formed (about 2 minutes). Bring milk to boil and add to the roux while stirring constantly. As soon as it is smooth, pour into the top part of a double saucepan. Then add Parmesan cheese, reserving 6 level tablespoons for later use, and leave over gently simmering water for about 20 minutes. Season to taste and keep warm. Viewers will have seen Malcolm Reid enrich this sauce by adding cream and Hollandaise Sauce (see below). This would be an optional luxury.

To assemble pancakes
Butter a large rectangular oven-proof dish. Fill each pancake generously with a few tablespoons of the spinach mixture and roll up, gently placing them side by side in the buttered dish. Place in a warm oven, gas mark 1, 275°F. When ready to serve, remove pancakes from oven; pour sauce over them and sprinkle with remaining grated Parmesan cheese. Place dish under grill until golden brown, hot and bubbling. Serve at once. Serves 6.

Hollandaise Sauce (optional)

2 tbsp white wine vinegar	3 egg yolks
3 tbsp water	6 oz unsalted butter
1 small piece onion	Lemon juice
6 peppercorns	Salt and freshly-ground
1 small piece bay leaf	white pepper

Put the butter into a small pan and stand this in a warm place to melt and get quite hot. Put the wine vinegar, water, onion, peppercorns and bay leaf into a small pan and boil rapidly until the mixture is reduced to 1 tablespoon.

Now add two more tablespoons of water (you require the

original quantity of liquid to extract the aromas in the first stage; you then need to replace some of the liquid which has evaporated).

Select a bowl which has a good round bottom and which will sit in the top of a pan of boiling water. Put the egg yolks into the bowl and strain the liquid on to them, stirring well with a tiny balloon whisk or spatula.

Arrange the bowl over the boiling water and whisk gently but completely, taking care to see that the egg doesn't set on the sides of the bowl.

Continue whisking until the mixture is thick and the whisk leaves a definite trail, but stop before the eggs scramble! (Have a container of cold water to hand as a safety precaution. Dip the base of the bowl into the water to remove the residual heat quickly, thus avoiding any possibility of the egg over-cooking).

Now stand the bowl on a folded damp cloth (this helps keep the bowl steady as you whisk). Whisk in a few drops only of the melted butter at first and as the sauce thickens add the butter more quickly until it is all incorporated (leave out the milky sediment which will have settled to the bottom of the pan whilst the butter has been slowly melting).

Adjust the seasoning, adding a little lemon juice and salt and pepper if you think it is needed. Squeeze little pieces of butter over the surface to prevent a crust forming. The butter can be whisked briskly into the sauce just before serving. Stand the sauce in a warm place until you are ready to use it.

As this is a warm sauce, it must not be kept where it is too hot or it will separate, so keep an eye on it. A good place to put it is on top of a plate which in turn is standing on top of a pan of hot, but not simmering, water.

Noisettes d'Agneau au Noilly

Noisettes of lamb*	Double cream
Finely chopped onion	Salt, pepper
Fresh rosemary	Butter
Noilly Prat Vermouth	

Sauté the cuts of lamb in butter, leaving them pink inside. Remove and keep warm. Add onion to pan with small amount of rosemary, and cook until transparent. Add Noilly Prat Vermouth and reduce the liquid by half. Add cream and reduce again until the liquid reaches a saucy consistency. Season with salt and freshly-milled pepper, then strain the pan sauce over the lamb. Garnish with watercress.

(*A 'noisette' is a luxurious cut of lamb, where only the 'eye' of the cutlet is used. An acceptable alternative is to ask your butcher to bone, skin, roll and tie a loin of lamb before cutting it into 1½-inch thick rounds. Allow 1 thick or 2 thin pieces per serving.)

Haricots Verts aux Fines Herbs

1½ lb (750 grms) French
    beans, blanched
4 tbsp olive or nut oil
1 finely-chopped onion
2 crushed cloves garlic
1 finely-chopped or
    grated carrot
3 tbsp brown stock

1 dsp each of finely-
    chopped parsley,
    tarragon, chives, chervil,
    basil and seasoning
Salt and pepper

Wash, top and tail the beans and cut them in half. Heat the oil in a heavy frying-pan and cook the onion, crushed garlic and carrot for approximately 5 minutes, or until the onion is golden.

Add the beans, stock and finely-chopped herbs. Season. (To make stock dissolve 1 stock cube in about one third of a pint of water.) Cover and cook for a further 5 minutes and then serve. Serves 5-6.

Tarte Amandine

Pastry
8 oz flour
4 oz butter
1 oz sugar

1 fl. oz water
Pinch salt

Filling
5 oz ground almonds
4 oz castor sugar
4 oz butter

2 eggs
Raspberry jam

Topping
1 egg white
8 oz icing sugar

Flaked almonds

Rub fat into the flour; add sugar; add water and salt and mix lightly. Line six 4-inch flan tins and spread raspberry jam on base.

Cream butter and sugar until almost white, add eggs and ground almonds and mix together. Spoon into the cases. Bake at gas mark 5, 375°F, until golden brown. (Approximately 30-35 minutes.)

Allow tarts to cool. Beat egg whites slightly and add icing sugar to make soft icing. Spread on top of tarts and cover with flaked almonds. Glaze in a hot oven until very lightly brown, and dust with icing sugar. Serve warm or cold. Serves 6.

NICO LADENIS

CHEZ NICO

People determined to eat excellent food will make the pilgrimage to South East London, where, in Lordship Lane, right opposite East Dulwich Police Station, they will find a very individual French restaurant called Chez Nico.

There is nothing spectacular about the place itself. In fact it is rather plain and has a functional appearance. This could not, however, be said of the owners, Nico and Diane Ladenis. It would be hard to find two more colourful and single-minded restaurateurs. The pair work in harmony and pay meticulous attention to minutiae; each spoon and fork is regimented, the linen is crisply creased, the bread always warmed, the butter chilled and of the finest quality and each wine caressingly served. In the kitchen each tempting sauce glistens on the plate — not too thick, not too thin, and timed to arrive at its peak.

Nico Ladenis, born in East Africa of French/Greek parents, is a strange but handsome figure; strange because he is much more robust than the customary image of a Frenchman. This could be due to his English education and his Yorkshire University training as an economist. Having been rejected by several industrial firms for failing their aptitude tests, he was advised not to work for others but to become his own boss. Surely this must have been one of the best pieces of advice ever given, and — fortunately for us, his customers — taken!

Dinah-Jane, or Diane as she is popularly called, is also French, but English bred. Her first approach to the customer, as front-of-house *directrice*, is authoritative but kind. Like the gentle teacher she is, she guides you firmly to the right solution when you are composing your menu, never allowing a second's hesitation, for to hesitate is to be lost in her eyes. A rare and remarkable understanding of human nature has been built up over the years. Because of her total trust and faith in her husband's culinary creations, her faultless knowledge of the day's market, her care with the wine list and her ability to understand her customers' quirks and social insecurities, it might be truly said she is London's safest and most accurate *maître d'hôtel*.

Nico, on the other hand, enjoys a drama in his kitchen. A simultaneous, boring order for two melons and two veal chops would be enough for him to leap the barrier 'twixt stove and table; but his wife now never allows such a situation to arise. Nico takes to customers warily, but once they have gained his confidence, and *vice versa*, they are allowed to infiltrate the inner sanctum near his kitchen, there to be entertained with descriptions of his latest culinary adventures and fascinated by the sharpness of his wit for he is a delightfully cynical raconteur.

Nico is tempted to move into London's West End and I know pressure is applied regularly, perhaps — dare I say? — by those who don't like making the journey to the South East. But to move might be foolhardy, for London's West End is, unlike the East, peopled by a tough bunch of folk which is prepared to change its loyalties at the drop of a fork. He might even be better employed further out in the provinces where the other chefs in this book enjoy a quality of life which the harassed Londoner is rarely privileged to experience but then *they* would have nowhere to dine when visiting our capital.

CHEZ NICO

Mousse de Saumon Fumé au Cresson
Carré d'Agneau aux Marrons
Sorbet aux Citrons Verts

Mousse de Saumon Fumé au Cresson

2 pints rich Béchamel Sauce
into which 3 tbsp of aspic
crystals melted in 3 tbsp
of water have been mixed
1 heaped tsp tomato purée
20 oz smoked salmon

2 cloves garlic, crushed
Juice and zest of 3 lemons
$\frac{3}{4}$ pint double cream
4 egg whites
A good pinch cayenne
pepper

Filling layer
Leaves from 3 bunches
watercress
3 shallots, finely chopped
$\frac{3}{4}$ lb white mushrooms,
chopped or sliced

2 oz butter
Salt, pepper

First make the filling. In a frying pan sauté the shallots in the butter. Add chopped mushrooms and cook together. Then add watercress, salt and pepper. Cook until the cress has 'wilted'. Then put into a blender and make a purée. Set aside to cool. Next liquidise salmon, Béchamel, lemon juice and zest and garlic, in two or three stages until very smooth. Beat double cream until just beginning to ribbon. Beat egg whites until semi-stiff. Mix double cream into salmon/Béchamel mixture. Then fold in the egg whites. Pour mixture into a mould to about half-way up. Place in freezer to set. Remove, and pour over the filling layer with the aid of a spatula. Spread evenly to same thickness all over. Pour the rest of the mixture over to reach to the top and return the mould to freezer until well set. Remove and place in refrigerator. Serve next day.

To serve the mousse: Overturn as follows. Run a knife all along the edges to the bottom. Place in very hot water for 15-20 seconds, and overturn onto a large platter. Slice with fish slicer, with great care. Garnish with sprigs of freshly-picked and washed watercress.

Carré d'Agneau aux Marrons

One best end of lamb (or
more) trimmed and ready
for cooking
1 clove garlic cut into slivers
Sarriette (wild savory)
Salt, pepper

Butter
Rich brown sauce with
Madeira
8 fresh chestnuts

21

Make slits between cutlets and insert thin slivers of garlic. Sprinkle with pepper (add salt later). Seal lightly on both sides in hot butter. Place on grill and cook for about 5 minutes on either side. Place in roasting pan, cover with butter, sprinkle with sarriette and roast to medium done — i.e. pink.

Meantime have ready 8 roasted chestnuts. After peeling, place in pan with some demi-glace sauce (see below) and heat through to a consistency where sauce is syrupy and coats the chestnuts. Slice best end of lamb into cutlets and sprinkle with parsley. Serve them and the chestnuts together on same plate, and present. Serves 2.

Brown Sauce

2 tbsp olive oil	2 oz flour
2 oz butter	1 small bay leaf
1 small onion	1 good pinch of thyme
1 4-inch carrot	1 tsp red currant jelly
1 celery stalk	4 oz Madeira
2 oz field mushrooms,	1½ pints water
chopped	Salt and freshly milled
2 tsp tomato purée	black pepper
1 chicken stock cube	

Heat oil and butter until lightly smoking. Allow chopped carrot, celery and onion to gradually brown in this. Add mushrooms and continue to fry over a medium heat. Add tomato purée and, watching carefully as the purée burns easily, allow everything to take on a little more colour. Lower heat, add flour, stir well in and allow to brown stirring from time to time to prevent sticking.

Add herbs now (do not add earlier or they will burn nd give a bitter taste). Add red currant jelly. Pour mixture into a clean dish whilst you pour into the frying pan the red wine. This will release any brown sediments on the bottom of the pan. Crumble in the stock cube. Return everything to the pan. Add the water, bring to the boil, adding a little salt and pepper.

Simmer for 30 minutes, stirring to prevent sticking. Strain the sauce into a clean pan (you should have about 1 pint of sauce when finished). Adjust seasoning with more salt if necessary. Cover with a circle of buttered paper and keep hot over simmering water until required. This sauce can be frozen in small quantities and kept until needed.

Sorbet aux Citrons Verts

1 Kiwi fruit
6 limes
½ pint syrup made from
   ¾ lb sugar and ½ pint
   water

5 egg whites
1 sachet gelatine
icing sugar

Peel the limes, avoiding the white pith, and add to sugar and water to make the syrup. Squeeze the peeled limes. Having boiled the water, sugar and lime peel together for 5 minutes, pour the lime juice into the hot syrup and put aside to cool. Before it is completely cool, dissolve the gelatine well and strain the whole lot into a sorbetière. Beat egg whites in a pan over light heat with some icing sugar until stiff. Scoop into the sorbetière and place in freezer compartment of refrigerator. In about one hour the sorbet should be ready. This keeps well in the freezer for several days and will never solidify or become icy but will remain fluffy. Serve in fluted glasses and place a slice of Kiwi on top.

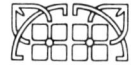

BRIAN SACK & FRANCIS COULSON

SHARROW BAY HOTEL

It is said that some thirty years ago a slim young ex-actor was seen pushing a bike laden with suitcases, pots, pans and a kettle, along the banks of Lake Ullswater towards the village of Pooley Bridge and onwards to a remote Victorian mansion where the lake's water laps the very edge of its garden. The man was Francis Coulson, and he was fleeing from a career in the London theatre. The house was Sharrow Bay, and it was his intention to start doing bed and breakfast and afternoon teas. Today, thirty years later, it might truly be said that The Sharrow Bay Country House Hotel is Britain's best hotel, and its restaurant one of the finest in the land, having already acquired the Hotel of the Year award in 1974 and many coveted stars from Britain's leading guides.

Francis Coulson's partner, Brian Sack, joined him some years later, when he felt he would like to escape from London, although he was a successful surveyor, and try his hand at buttering toast and serving scones. He wanted to see if he, too, could take to hotel keeping. As a result an internationally-known partnership was formed.

The twosome have gone from strength to strength and anyone lucky enough to have been a guest in their house (for that is how they intend you should feel) will know what a welcome awaits you as you step through the door.

Francis is a man after my own heart in that he loves food, and excels at making puddings and pies and pastries, and *real* custard from eggs and cream, and exotically-flavoured mousses. The 'dessert' menu at Sharrow Bay is thoroughly satisfying. It often includes a typically English pudding which arrives bathed in thick fresh cream.

Visitors to fine resturants always need encouragement to try new dishes, and it is here that Brian Sack comes into his own. Looking like a benign doctor, and immaculately clad in a tailored suit, he approaches each table peering over half-specs. 'Just a half portion, perhaps?' he says. It is impossible to refuse, and as you succumb, he smiles indulgently.

Francis Coulson, a behind-the-scenes man, ensures that every dish leaving his kitchens is at its peak when it arrives at your table. The staff, most of whom have been at Sharrow Bay for many years, are as keen to serve you as are their employers and both Francis and Brian are quick to point out that without their loyalty Sharrow Bay might not be what it is today. I doubt that.

Many have tried to emulate Sharrow Bay, but few have succeeded in spite of their insistence that 'anyone can do it'. But if someone — you perhaps? — if you were *really* determined, well, who knows?

SHARROW BAY HOTEL

Avocado Mousse
Lamb Chops in Puff Pastry
Aubergines – Sharrow Style
Roesti Potatoes
Vanilla Bavarian Cream
Sticky Toffee Pudding

Avocado Mousse

2 ripe avocado pears,
  peeled and pitted
$\frac{1}{2}$ pint mayonnaise
$\frac{1}{2}$ pint double cream,
  whipped
$\frac{1}{2}$ tbsp lemon juice

$\frac{1}{4}$-$\frac{1}{2}$ oz gelatine in 2 tbsp
  water
1 tsp onion juice
Seasoning (salt, pepper,
  sugar, Worcester sauce,
  according to taste)

Liquidise the peeled pears and mix well in to the mayonnaise. Add the lemon and onion juice, seasoning to taste with salt, pepper, a little sugar and a dash of Worcester sauce.

Dissolve the gelatine in the water in bowl placed over a pan of boiling water. Stir this into the mixture before incorporating the whipped cream.

Pour the mixture into pots and chill until set. The mousse can be garnished with dressed prawns and swirls of unsweetened whipped cream. Serves 5-6.

Lamb Chops in Puff Pastry

12 lamb chops, well
  trimmed of skin and fat
Home-made puff pastry (or
  1 large packet frozen)

Beaten egg

Stuffing
Half a cucumber
1 onion, very finely
  chopped
1 oz butter
1 oz fresh white
  breadcrumbs

1 egg, beaten
1 heaped tbsp freshly
  chopped mint
Squeeze of lemon juice
Salt and milled pepper

Peel, de-seed and finely chop the cucumber. Fry the chopped onion in the butter until quite soft but *not* brown. Stir in the breadcrumbs, bind with the egg. Mix the cucumber in, add the mint, and season well with salt, pepper and lemon. (More mint can be added to taste.)

Quickly grill or fry each chop on each side. They should be nicely browned, but pink inside. Leave these to cool, retaining the pan juices if you want to make a little gravy.

Roll out the pastry thinly, cut into 12 squares big enough to wrap each chop in. Cut a template with a piece of paper.

27

Now, press a goodly cushion of stuffing on the eye of each chop. Enfold in the thinly-rolled pastry squares, brush with beaten egg and arrange on a baking sheet.

Bake at gas mark 7, 425° F, until the pastry is crisp and golden-brown.

Gravy

Pour excess fat away from frying-pan, leaving about 2 tablespoons. Stir a dessertspoonful of flour into the pan juices. Add a teaspoonful of tomato purée. Brown gently over a low heat. Add half pint of veal or chicken stock. Simmer for 20 minutes, skimming off any surplus fat. Season carefully, adding a few bruised mint leaves and a modicum of crushed garlic. Strain and serve separately.

Aubergines — Sharrow Style

3 medium aubergines	1 oz Cheddar cheese
6 tomatoes, skinned and de-seeded	Sprinkling Parmesan cheese
1 tsp thyme	2 cloves
1 clove garlic (optional)	Salt, pepper
chopped chives	Oil

Slice the aubergines, season with salt and pepper and press in a colander with a heavy weight to remove excess water.

Heat oil, add minced garlic, cloves, thyme and chives and add the aubergines, frying quickly. Place in an ovenproof casserole with tomatoes. Sprinkle with the Cheddar and Parmesan cheese. Cook in oven until brown and put under the grill (to glaze) with a little extra cheese. Serves 5-6.

Roesti Potatoes

Parboil four large potatoes. Allow to cool. Peel. Grate on coarse grater. Peel and chop one onion. Sauté in butter until tender, put aside. (If liked, add a minced clove of garlic.) In a frying-pan, or two smaller flat pans, heat a mixture of butter and lard to coat the base of the pan. When hot, add half of the grated potato, then put the sautéed onion on top, finishing off with the rest of the potato, i.e. make a sandwich of your sautéed potatoes. Fry on hot stove. When brown, turn, and fry second side also until crisp and brown. To serve, cut into wedge shapes. Serves 5-6.

Vanilla Bavarian Cream

1 pint milk	1 pint cream
8 egg yolks	4 level tsp powdered
8 oz sugar	gelatine
Two vanilla pods or a little	A little cold water
vanilla essence	Fresh raspberries

Bring milk up to the boil with vanilla pods or vanilla essence. Meanwhile separate the eggs. Whip the yolks and sugar to a light creamy texture. Add the milk. Stir the milk, egg yolks and sugar mixture over a low heat until just under the boil (until coating the back of a wooden spoon). Test by dipping your finger in and seeing that the mixture leaves a trail. Place two tablespoons of cold water in a pan, add gelatine and stir over a low heat until transparent. *Do not boil.* Add to mixture, stirring in very thoroughly. Place in refrigerator. When cool and on the point of setting, whisk cream to the same consistency and fold in. Place in pots and allow to set. Serve topped with fresh raspberries.

This recipe can be varied by selecting different flavourings such as rum, coffee, Grand Marnier, etc.

Sticky Toffee Pudding
(This recipe is being included by popular request.)

2 oz softened butter	$\frac{1}{2}$ pint boiling water
6 oz granulated sugar	1 tsp bicarbonate of soda
$\frac{1}{2}$ lb flour	1 tsp vanilla essence
1 tsp baking powder	$2\frac{1}{2}$ oz brown sugar
1 egg	$1\frac{1}{2}$ oz butter
6 oz stoned dates	2 tbsp double cream

Cream the butter and sugar together. Sift the flour and baking powder. Beat the whisked egg into the creamed mixture with some of the flour. Continue beating for a minute or so before mixing in the rest of the flour.

Flour the dates lighly and chop them finely. Pour the boiling water over them. Mix in the bicarbonate of soda and vanilla. Add this mixture to the batter and blend well. Turn it into a buttered cake tin (11 inches by 7 inches). Bake for about 40 minutes in a moderate oven, gas mark 5, 375° F.

For the toffee coating, heat the brown sugar, butter and cream and simmer for 3 minutes. Pour over the hot pudding and place under a hot grill until it bubbles. N.B. the coating burns easily.

MICHEL ROUX

THE WATERSIDE INN

It would have been impossible to produce a book on the best cooks in England and not to have included the famous Roux brothers. And yet, how do they fit into our scheme? They seem to be 'professionals', while the other candidates are, as I said in the Foreword, 'amateurs' who started as something other than cooks. But, in fact, the Roux brothers did not start life as restaurateurs, though they now control a mighty empire.

Michel carries the highest awards his native France can give, from Maître Patissier de France in 1963 to the unusual honour of 'Meilleur Ouvrier' de France in 1976. Whilst both brothers come from a professional background — their father was a *pâtissier* in Paris — neither had a formal hotel school training. Albert Henri Roux joined the kitchen team at our own Embassy in Paris after his apprenticeship under his father. Michel André Roux, the 'kid brother', joined him there and trained under him. So, though they served an apprenticeship, neither had been trained in a restaurant.

By the 1960s they were working independently in England for such illustrious families as the Rothschilds, the Clores and the Cazalets. Then, in April 1967 they decided to join forces. Le Gavroche, in London's Lower Sloane Street, was their first joint venture. It was an overnight success. Within six months it was acclaimed by the British gastronomic press to be the best French restaurant to open in London since the war. Before two years had passed it had achieved international fame, and stars were showered upon it by the food critics.

The Poulbot, near St Paul's Cathedral in the City, began in 1969 to provide the kind of food at lunchtime that Le Gavroche was supplying to the well-heeled in Chelsea for dinnertime. In 1971 this City restaurant won the coveted Egon Ronay Gold Plate Award as restaurant of the year — a reward for hard work, because the Roux brothers were now cooking for lunch in the City, and dinner in Chelsea.

Recognising that there was now a need for a middle-priced, lively establishment led them to their third venture, Le Gamin in Old Bailey. Again they created an excellent restaurant without letting standards fall at the other establishments. Poulbot and Gamin for lunch, then a quick trip to Sloane Street to apply their personal touch in the evenings at Le Gavroche for dinner.

Gluttons for work, Michel and Albert found themselves kicking their heels on Sundays. So, in 1972, to take care of this 'floating' day they purchased 'a simple English country pub', the Waterside Inn at Bray near Windsor, where willow trees waft in the breeze, ducks and swans sail past the dining-room windows and diners can enjoy an hour or two of French atmosphere and French food.

The style of Waterside's dining-room can hardly be equated with that of a simple English inn. The scheme is as delicate and subtle as the Thames landscape outside. The tables are decked in crisp linen. The elegant china, glass and cutlery sparkles, the swagged blinds hanging at the vast panoramic windows give the place a chic atmosphere reminiscent of a French château. Not a word of English passes the lips of the staff. Chauvinism? Perhaps, but it works. As we British say, the proof of the pudding is in the eating. And, of course, the restaurants are separated only by a drive down the M4 so that Michel can 'mount' a sauce in Bray and finish a soufflé in Chelsea!

THE WATERSIDE INN

Saucisson de Volaille Bonnefoy
Entrecôte Canaille
Gratin Savoyard
Soufflé Framboise

Saucisson de Volaille Bonnefoy

6 chicken breasts (including the tip of the wing bone)
Chicken stock (made from carcass bones)

Aspic jelly made either by clarifying some of the chicken stock; or use a commercial brand.

Stuffing
4 oz raw lean ham
4 oz boned chicken leg-meat
2 tbsp thick cream
1 egg

Salt, pepper
2 truffles (optional)

Carefully fold back the 'fillet' on each breast without detaching it from the rest of the meat. With a wetted cutlet bat (or milk bottle) very gently flatten the breasts.

Mince together the ham and chicken leg-meat. Put into a blender with the beaten egg, salt and pepper, blend until a fine purée is obtained. Add the finely chopped truffles (if used) and stir in the cream.

Divide into six portions and arrange a 'sausage' of this forcemeat down the centre of the breasts. Brush the edges with beaten egg white, then fold over and form into sausage shapes. Tie each sausage tightly in a piece of muslin. Poach in lightly-seasoned chicken stock for 20 minutes. Leave to cool completely in the liquid.

Cut the breasts into oblique slices and arrange in an oval dish. Coat with aspic; refrigerate until set. Serve with a French bean salad. Serves 6.

Entrecôte Canaille

6 entrecôtes — 8-10 oz each when trimmed
4 shallots
$\frac{1}{4}$ pt tarragon vinegar
$\frac{1}{4}$ pt dry white wine
$\frac{1}{2}$ pt double cream

Chervil, fresh tarragon

Cook the entrecôtes to your liking. Put them on a dish and keep in a warm place. Take excess fat from the pan and add the finely-chopped shallots. Add vinegar and white wine. Let reduce. Add cream, chopped chervil and tarragon. Cook until thickish. Cover the entrecôtes with this sauce and serve. Serves 6.

Gratin Savoyard

Finely slice potatoes and sauté in a pan with butter until they are thoroughly cooked. Drain them. Cook again with cream for a few minutes. Add salt and pepper. Then arrange in an oven-proof dish. Add cheese (Gruyère) on the top and glaze under a hot grill. Serves 6.

Soufflé Framboise

Crème Pâtissière
9 fluid oz milk (scant half-pint)

3 egg yolks
2 oz castor sugar
1 oz plain flour

Other Ingredients
½ lb raspberries (fresh or frozen)

2 oz castor sugar
2 fluid oz water

Garnish
4 oz raspberries (soaked in Framboise liqueur, raspberry 'alcohol' or gin)

1½ oz crushed almond macaroons
6 egg whites

Have ready a well-buttered 3-pint soufflé dish.

Now make the pastry cream by blending the yolks, sugar and flour until smooth and creamy. Bring the milk to the boil, pour over the mixture stirring all the time. Return the pan to a low heat and whisk until thick: do not boil. Leave to cool.

Next, make the raspberry purée by cooking the ½ lb of raspberries, sugar and water until jam-like. Sieve and leave to cool. Mix the above two mixtures together. Have ready the fresh or de-frosted raspberries and the lightly crushed macaroons. Beat 6 egg whites until stiff.

Take two spoonfuls of this and mix well into the basic preparation. Gently fold and cut in the remaining beaten egg whites. Put one-third of the mixture into the soufflé dish, then a layer of raspberries, then the next third of the mixture, then a layer of crushed macaroons, and then the rest of the mixture, levelling-off the top and cleaning the edge of the dish. Now run the point of a knife round the edge of the mixture, about ¼ inch in from the rim.

Stand the soufflé in a shallow pan of gently simmering water for 5 minutes, after which time you will see it start to 'move'. Transfer the soufflé to a preheated oven, gas mark 6,

400° F, for 25-30 minutes, when the soufflé will have risen but still be moist inside.

Serve hot with warm raspberry sauce.

Raspberry Sauce

8 oz fresh or frozen	3 oz castor sugar
raspberries	2 tbsps gin or water
Juice of 1 lemon	

Bring all the ingredients to the boil over a very low heat. Simmer gently for 5 minutes and then very gently press the contents through a fine sieve, applying only a minimum of pressure to the fruit so that the sauce remains clear. If you wish you can serve the sauce without sieving.

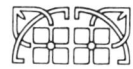

KENNETH BELL

THORNBURY CASTLE

When you first meet Kenneth Bell he may seem slightly melancholy. But when he begins to hold forth on the subjects of food, wine and history, a light comes into his eyes and enthusiasm into his voice. He belongs more to the traditional past than to the second half of the twentieth century. He is a man of infinite kindness who gently offers you his philosophy by means of his cooking, his viniculture and, not least, the atmosphere of his magnificent castle at Thornbury. Kenneth Bell is only the fifth owner of this great edifice from whose towers you can see almost the length and breadth of the Severn Estuary from Bristol to St George's Channel.

He feels that a guest needs only a quiet blue cloth, a simple knife and fork, spoon and plate and, very important, a full-bellied glass with which to catch the 'nose' of whichever wine he may choose. It could be his own fresh-flavoured 'Thornbury' with its light German tones or a rich Burgundy from vineyards whose history is similar to that of his own castle, or an elegant claret from a medieval château in south-west France.

His meticulous kitchen is, by many standards, modest in size and almost devoid of modern equipment. It is run virtually single-handed, because Kenneth Bell's philosophy is 'small and flawless is beautiful'. But this, of course, does not apply to his castle!

Years ago he abandoned his training as an engineer and, after the war, went as a student to the famous Ecole Hôtelière in Lausanne, where he told me, 'You learnt little about cooking but, you certainly learnt how to work!' Then in Oxford, he embarked on his first venture, 'The Elizabeth', which was an immediate success. He insists that his cooking then was more robust than it is today, gutsy with perhaps too much garlic and tomato purée — and indeed this was typical of most aspiring cooks in the early 1950s when 'good food' was just beginning to appear in England. 'The Elizabeth' is there to this day, for he sold it to his head waiter. But then travel broadened his outlook. And classical French cooking became his ambition.

Whether he fell in love with Thornbury Castle for its architectural splendour or because it offered the space to plant his 2000 vines, or both, is difficult to decide. In any case, he immediately encountered a major problem. This was solid rock only inches below the surface of what he had thought was suitable soil for nurturing vines. After an all-out attack with pneumatic drills today's bright green carpet of vines in front of Thornbury's grand façade began to flourish.

Simplicity became the trademark of his cooking. Excellence of raw materials (not least those from his abundant herb garden), good butter, cream and brandy have now almost superseded garlic, purée and spices.

To visit Thornbury is an enchanting experience which is enriched by the pervading sense of history. But Kenneth Bell stresses almost vehemently that it must be a 'night out'. If wearing your new frock creates a sense of occasion, then that's enough for him. He knows that once at his table all the nuances of his cooking plus the bouquet of his wines and the magic of the setting will make you want to return and learn more about the art of cooking from this master chef.

THORNBURY CASTLE

Inlayd Sill
Poulet Sauté au Vieux Vinaigre du Vin
Gratin Dauphinois
Ananas au Vin Rouge

Inlagd Sill

6 mackerel

Marinade

2 fluid oz white wine vinegar	1 tsp salt
1 medium-sized onion, finely chopped	Juice 1 lemon
	Dry cider
1 oz castor sugar	1 level tbsp chopped fresh
1 level tsp ground allspice	dill and parsley, or as
$\frac{1}{2}$ tsp ground black pepper	much as you like.

Clean and wash 6 mackerel, cut off heads and tails and split them in half horizontally. Remove backbone and fins; remove the majority of large bones (small ones will dissolve in the marinade). Cut the fillets into postage-stamp-sized cubes and lay them in a deep dish. Cover the fish with the above marinade, making up if necessary with dry cider so that it covers all the mackerel. Put in a cool place and stir occasionally to ensure that all pieces are in contact with the marinade. Marinade the fish for 36 to 48 hours. Six hours *is* sufficient but then it is a bit raw. The fish will keep in the marinade in a refrigerator for a week or more, but the flesh becomes a bit tough after three days.

Poulet Sauté au Vieux Vinaigre du Vin

1 roasting chicken cut
   into 8 serving portions
Olive or nut oil for frying
1 tbsp tomato purée
1 medium onion ⎫ cut into
2 medium carrots ⎬ $\frac{1}{4}$-inch
2 large stalks of celery ⎭ cubes
1 clove garlic chopped
1 sprig fresh or
   dried thyme
1 small bunch fresh or
   dried tarragon
2 fluid oz (scant $\frac{1}{4}$ pint)
   old red wine vinegar
1 tbsp brown sugar
$\frac{1}{2}$ bottle full-bodied
   red (cooking) wine

$\frac{1}{4}$ pint very strong
   fresh chicken stock
   or stock made from
   $\frac{1}{4}$ pint water to 1
   stock cube
A little beurre manié
   paste (1 oz softened
   butter blended with
   1 oz flour)
Salt, pepper

Pour a teacupful of oil into a heavy-bottomed sauté or frying-pan. Let the oil get to smoking heat. Brown the chicken pieces a few at a time, taking each piece out as it becomes well coloured. (There will be much spluttering as you go through this process, so take care and keep sleeves down and your face well out of the way.)

Now lower the heat and add the tomato purée, the carrots, celery and onion. Stir well and allow to fry for a minute or two. Add the garlic and herbs. Put the chicken pieces back into the pan, pour over the vinegar and allow to sizzle and reduce. Now add the sugar, red wine and stock. Season with salt and pepper and simmer until the breast pieces are tender. Take these out into a warm serving dish, leaving the leg pieces to cook until they too are tender, then remove them.

Now reduce the sauce by a third. Check the seasoning and thicken if necessary with little bits of beurre manié. Put the chicken pieces back into the sauce to re-heat if necessary.

Serve with pâté-spread fried croûtons or pastry crescents and the added luxury of a liberal sprinkling of freshly-chopped tarragon leaves.

Gratin Dauphinois

Chop quarter to half a clove of garlic *very* finely and scatter it over the bottom of a gratin dish. Peel 4 medium-sized potatoes and cut into neat slices the thickness of a 10p coin. Lay these neatly in the gratin dish, season with salt, pepper and a very little nutmeg, and just cover with thin cream or thick cream diluted with milk. Cook in a very slow oven for at least 1½ hours. If the oven is too hot the cream will separate — in which case shake the dish to amalgamate the liquids and turn the heat down. Serves 4.

Ananas au Vin Rouge

Cut a ripe pineapple into neat slices. Trim the slices of core and skin, lay them in a deep serving dish together with a stick of cinnamon and sprinkle with castor sugar. Pour over half a bottle of cheap red wine and leave to marinade for 6 hours. Add a little kirsch if you like it. Serve as it is.

THE HORN OF PLENTY

Sonia and Patrick Stevenson opened the doors of The Horn of Plenty near Tavistock in Devon on 12 May 1967. They did not barrage the neighbourhood with advertisements; they restricted themselves to a simple announcement that they were open and would remain open in the winter months, which is most unusual in Devon.

Within a year, Egon Ronay had given them two much-coveted stars and the *Good Food Guide* had also praised them.

Things had begun very differently for Sonia and her husband. She was a good classical violinist, and it was whilst she was playing professionally that she met Patrick, who had been employed working for the Southern Railway Company before entering the world of classical music as an opera singer. The decision to open a restaurant was taken simply because Sonia cooked so well. But this was not always the case. Patrick nevertheless revels in telling how Sonia, who was almost his child-bride, marched into Barker's butchery department and asked for a *whole* leg of beef! 'How many is this leg for?' the kindly butcher asked. 'Two,' was Sonia's naive reply. Her training had begun.

After twenty years as man and wife, and twelve as restaurateurs, they now bask in praise from England and abroad. In 1974 they were one of the 'original four' to be given that hitherto unattainable star by the *Guide Michelin*, France's top guide. Three years later they received the Restaurant of the Year Gold Plate Award from Egon Ronay, and Sonia became the first woman ever to prepare a dish in the kitchens of the famous Paris restaurant, Maxim's, when the Egon Ronay food guide was launched in that auspicious establishment. Last year Egon Ronay gave them the highest award it is possible to get in this country by adding a third star.

The Horn of Plenty itself nestles in the mountainside just off the A.390. A drive sweeps up to a rather dull portico and a more unpretentious place you will rarely find. The house relies totally on its natural setting. But after each car has rolled up the drive, and the occupants have descended and rung the bell, the large front door is swung open by a friendly young local lady. Once inside, the visitor finds a totally different atmosphere. This is unmistakably French,

SONIA STEVENSON

from the immense bunch of gladioli to the functional positioning of the tables in the glass-verandaed dining-room with its double glazing and its unique view of the valley below. The tables are broad and the chairs deep and ample. Patrick, whose bark is worse than his bite, looms over you like a bear as he guides, or rather bullies, you into your choice of dishes, and appropriate wines. Green-clad ladies then move swiftly around the tables, anticipating your every wish, from iced water to unsalted or salted butter. Perhaps the choice of an exclusively female staff is another of the secrets of The Horn of Plenty's success. Patrick Stevenson claims that local lasses are adaptable, efficient and a deal more friendly than their London male counterparts.

You will be lucky if you catch a glimpse of Sonia herself in her functional cook's outfit of vaguely surgical aspect. Should she appear at the end of the evening without her white head bandeau and neckerchief, you will discover a pretty, smiling and contented lady, pleased and even slightly embarrassed that she has satisfied your palate so well. Patrick looks equally contented as he bullies you into taking a glass of good vintage port with which to end a perfect evening.

THE HORN OF PLENTY

Duck Pâté
Quenelles de Mousseline de Saumon
Walnut Charlotte

Duck Pâté

One 5-6 lb duck
¾ lb minced pork
½ lb pork fat
2 tbsp brandy
1 oz butter
4 tbsp chopped shallots
¼ pint port

Salt, pepper
Allspice
Nutmeg
Chopped thyme and a finely-
 chopped clove of garlic
Aspic jelly to glaze

Slit the duck down the back and bone it, removing the fillets from the inside of the breast and some of the flesh from the more generously endowed part of the leg, but leaving the skin intact and still lined with meat. Cook the shallots gently in the butter, without letting them brown. Add the port and simmer until reduced by about half. Mix together well the minced veal, pork and pork fat and add the shallots and the reduced port. Season with salt, pepper, allspice, nutmeg and thyme and the finely-chopped garlic (remember that a cold dish needs more seasoning than a hot one).

Lay the duck skin out flat, sprinkle with a little more salt and with the brandy and spread with the stuffing mixture — arranging the strips of pork fat in the centre to make an attractive pattern when sliced. Re-form the duck and sew up. Roast for about 1½ hours in a very moderate oven, gas mark 2, 300° F. Cool, glaze and serve on a dish, decorated with chicory and orange.

This recipe is best made with a duck which has not been gutted. Bones, guts and all can be lifted out in one operation and no second slit need be made.

Quenelles de Mousseline de Saumon

1 lb raw salmon flesh
6 egg whites
1 pint lightly-beaten
 double cream

Salt, white pepper

Purée the salmon with the egg whites in a liquidiser. Press through a fine sieve. Add salt, pepper and fold in the cream. Chill. When you wish to serve the quenelles, place a flat pan of boiling salted water on to simmer.

Fill a warm dessertspoon with the chilled salmon mixture. Dip another warm dessertspoon in the boiling water and invert it over the first spoon to mould an oval-shaped

44

quenelle. Poach gently for 8 to 10 minutes until firm but still slightly creamy in the centre. Drain and serve with the following sauce poured over them.

Sauce au Vin Blanc

6 lb white fish bones,
    preferably turbot or sole
Cold water
2 tbsp of finely-chopped
    onions or shallots
1 oz butter

½ pint dry white wine
¾ pint double cream
Salt, pepper
Beurre manié
(1½ tbsp flour worked into
1½ tbsp butter)

Put fish bones in a large saucepan and cover with cold water. Bring to the boil, simmer for 10 minutes, then strain and simmer again till very well reduced and well flavoured.

Melt the butter and cook the onions gently in it until soft and transparent. Add the wine and simmer until reduced by about half. Add 1 pint of fish stock and the cream and bring, stirring, to the boil. Add the beurre manié in little pieces and simmer till it has dissolved and thickened the sauce. Season to taste and leave the sauce to 'mature' for 10 minutes. Then check for flavour and seasoning.

Walnut Charlotte

1 lb unsalted Dutch butter
10 egg yolks
10 oz sieved icing sugar
10 oz walnuts pulverised
    in an electric blender

Langue de chat biscuits
    (flat sponge fingers)
Walnut halves
Whipped cream to decorate

Cream the butter well. Add the lightly-beaten egg yolks and cream together again. Add the sieved icing sugar. Blend in the liquidised walnuts. Turn into a cake tin with a removable base, the sides lined with the *langue de chat* biscuits, and chill. When quite set, lift out and cover the top with whipped cream and decorate with walnut halves.

EGON RONAY'S COMMENTS AND RESTAURANT DETAILS

Here is a personal appraisal of the seven restaurants written by Egon Ronay especially for this book. These comments are not to be read as an official ranking of the restaurants.

White Moss House
There are regrettably few restaurants in England where they serve English dishes of quality, other than plain roasts and grills. Mrs Butterworth provides a genuine taste of England with dishes that sustain the promise of their names, such as artichoke and scallop soup, venison and game pasty with pickled damsons, and much more besides.

Jean and Arthur Butterworth
White Moss House
Rydal Water
Grasmere
English Lakes LA 22 9SA
Tel: (096-65) 295

The Box Tree Restaurant
Malcolm Reid and Colin Long are among the brilliant small band of dedicated people who, with no professional training, have created restaurants outstanding by any criteria. Innate good taste and fanatical interest in good food seem to be the two main qualities behind their success.

Malcolm Reid and Colin Long
The Box Tree Restaurant
Church Street
Ilkley
W Yorks
Tel: (0943) 608484

Chez Nico
Our inspectors are always happy, in wandering through the gastronomic deserts of south-east London, to arrive at the oasis of French cuisine provided by Mr and Mrs Ladenis. Good ingredients are served up with flair and inventiveness.

Nico and Diane Ladenis
Chez Nico
148 Lordship Lane
East Dulwich
London SE22
Tel: (01) 693-8266

The Sharrow Bay Hotel
A dinner cooked by Francis Coulson is an occasion worth the 300-mile journey from London, while a banquet prepared by Britain's best chefs is ideally crowned by Francis Coulson's sweets.

Francis Coulson and Brian Sack
The Sharrow Bay Hotel
Pooley Bridge
Lake Ullswater
Penrith
Cumbria CA10 2LZ
Tel: Pooleybridge (085-36) 301

The Waterside Inn
This is the third of the Roux brothers' restaurants, and my esteem for their excellence as chefs and restaurateurs is reflected in the fact that they are the only proprietors in Britain (outside the Savoy hotel group) who have three restaurants starred in our Guide.

Michel Roux
The Waterside Inn
Ferry Road
Bray
Berkshire
Tel: (0628) 20691/22941

Le Gavroche
61 — 63 Lower Sloane Street
London SW1
Tel: (01) 730 2820

Thornbury Castle
I have admired Kenneth Bell's cooking since I first encountered it at the Elizabeth in Oxford about 20 years ago. Now in his castle on the Severn he has created, in an old English setting, the excellent French provincial type of restaurant he always aspired to, where I would always happily return for his wonderful salmon in pastry, among other expert dishes.

Kenneth Bell
Thornbury Castle
Thornbury
Bristol 12 1HH
Tel: (0454) 41-2647

The Horn of Plenty
Sonia Stevenson has few peers of either sex in the culinary arts. Entirely self-taught, though inspired by her partner-husband, she seems able to achieve success in any dish she tackles; her repertoire is immense, and her inventiveness with ingredients is masterly.

Sonia and Patrick Stevenson
The Horn of Plenty
Gullworthy
Nr Tavistock
Devon
Tel: Gunnislake (0822) 832528

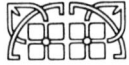